make me I'm yours...

Party

D&C

David and Charles

www.rucraft.co.uk

contents

Cards and Gifts

Techniques

introduction

What better way to celebrate a special occasion with those you love – friends, family and neighbours – than with decorations, gifts and treats that you have made yourself. And, by making your own party garlands, dinner table settings, gift wrappings and celebration cakes, you can even save a tidy little sum. Even the cash-strapped can throw a fabulous party on a budget with the wealth of ideas on offer here.

This book has over 20 great reasons to discover how much fun crafts can be, from simple sewn celebration bunting to pretty paper-sculpted tiaras and gift bags. And for those with a sweet tooth, there are gift-shaped iced cookies and stunning sugarpaste cakes. Each project has been rated to give you an idea of just how easy it is to make.

These are the simplest of projects to get you started on discovering the great crafts featured.

Easing you in, these projects will help you to explore your newfound talents and creative inclinations.

As your passion for crafting grows, these designs will help you to round out developing skills.

The 'tips and tricks' running throughout the book will give you ideas for adapting the projects whatever your celebration – from baby showers to birthdays, christenings to Christmas, and so many more besides.

party
accents

paper lanterns

These brightly coloured lanterns make wonderful party decorations and, as they are made from fairly thick handmade paper, they hold their shape even once cut. Inspired by the Far East, they can be hung from a pagoda for a summer garden party; alternatively, make them on a smaller scale and string together in garlands for indoor gatherings. However, they're not intended for use as lampshades with light bulbs, and shouldn't be used as such!

you will need (for the blue lantern) ...

- A2 (16½ x 23⅜in) sheet of decorative blue handmade paper

- A4 (US letter) sheets of pink and green handmade paper

- zigzag scissors

- florists' wire

- flat-head pliers

- coordinating ribbon for hanging

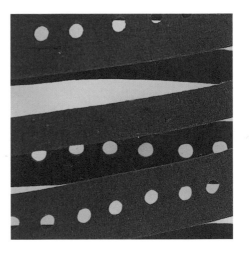

1. Cut a 45 x 28cm (17⅝ x 11in) rectangle of the blue paper. Lightly score a line every 11cm (4¼in) to divide it into four panels. The last score line will leave a narrow border 1cm (⅜in) wide. Gently fold the paper along the score lines. Fold under the border and glue it under the opposite side to create the cuboid shape. Flatten the lantern in half.

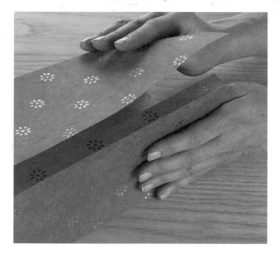

2. Very lightly draw a vertical line 2.5cm (1in) to the right of each fold. Starting 2cm (¾in) down from the top of the lantern, mark lines 1cm (⅜in) apart, from the pencil line to the fold. Stop 2cm (¾in) above the lower edge of the lantern. Keeping the paper folded, cut along the pencil lines to make tabs. Repeat at each fold.

3. Flatten each corner then very lightly score the sides of every other tab on both sides of the fold, starting at the top.

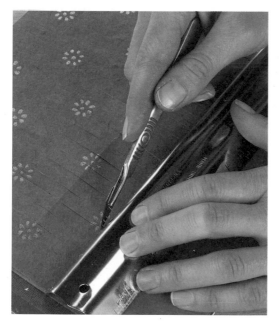

4. Cut two 2cm (¾in) wide strips of pink paper with zigzag scissors. Glue a strip around the top and bottom edges of the lantern. Cut two thin strips of green paper and glue these along the centres of the pink borders.

5. Once the borders are dry, fold each corner again. Starting at the top of the lantern, push alternate tabs inwards, towards the centre of the lantern, to make a step pattern.

6. To make a hanger, cut an 18cm (7in) length of florists' wire. Wrap the middle of the wire around a pencil and twist to make a loop. Pierce a hole at two opposite corners of the top of the lantern. Poke the ends of the wires through the holes and curl up the very ends with a pair of pliers. Tie a length of coordinating ribbon from the centre of the hanger to suspend the lantern.

Tips and Tricks

The pink lantern is made in the same way as the blue one, but the cylinders of paper are cut and scored differently, varying the width of the strips for different effects.

For Halloween, make your lanterns from coloured foil or acetate to reflect candlelight.

For a silver wedding anniversary, try making simple round lanterns from silver lacy doilies.

At Christmas string garlands of tiny lanterns on the tree.

cupcake napkin

To make your party extra special, why not have a go at making and embellishing your own serviettes? These elegant linen napkins are appliquéd with tasty cupcakes cut from colourful fabric scraps, and finished with vibrant emerald-green ric-rac. The fabric scraps have been carefully chosen to represent the cupcake – these include a pretty striped cotton for the icing and a red and white polka-dot fabric for the cherry.

you will need (for one napkin) ...

- 37cm (14½in) square white linen
- 152cm (60in) ric-rac
- selection of fabric scraps
- fusible web

1. The napkin has traditional mitred corners – a sophisticated way to finish off the corners by enclosing all the raw edges. Working from the front of your fabric, press under 1cm (⅜in) around the entire square. Press under a further 2cm (¾in) to create your hem. To mitre the corners, open out the pressed seams and, on the 2cm (¾in) fold line, insert a pin at the corners.

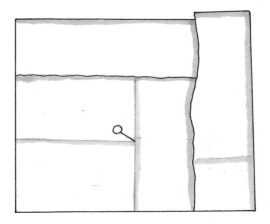

2. Make a crease diagonally at this point and score along the fold line with your fingernail (pressing with the iron will press out the existing fold lines).

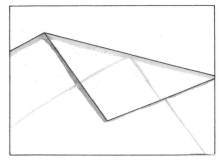

3. Refold the hems and pin into position at the mitres and every 5cm (2in). Topstitch close to the folded edge, taking care at the corners. Slipstitch the mitre into place.

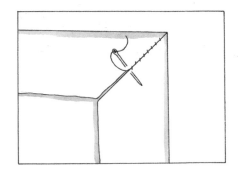

4. Pin and stitch the ric-rac over your stitching line to hide the seams.

5. Draw out the sections of the cupcake template onto the fusible web, fuse to your chosen fabrics and cut out. Fuse onto the napkin diagonally at one corner using a pressing cloth to avoid marking the linen. (Note some of the sections need to be fused onto each other to build up the design.)

6. Machine appliqué the cupcake design in place – this will take patience and time, as you need to go around fairly intricate shapes and will need to change threads for each fabric. As long as you have a good zigzag stitch on your machine, you can keep the bobbin threaded with ivory thread and only change the needle thread.

Tips and Tricks

Why not choose your own motifs? Just remember to keep your shapes simple, using no more than four colours for each!

For a summer garden party, choose flowers, snails and butterflies.

For Christmas gatherings, a gingerbread man is a great decoration.

elegant garlands

Simple paper shapes make the most unexpected forms if they are joined together in multiples. Semicircles cut from decorative Japanese papers are joined in groups of six to create stylized flower-like forms. Eye pins have been inserted through the decorations so that they can be strung together to make a garland, and the pins have been threaded with some small pearly beads in colours to coordinate with the papers.

you will need ...

- A4 (US letter) sheets of handmade patterned papers in pale colours
- large and small pale pink and green pearl beads
- metal eye pins
- embroidery thread or thin wire
- round-nose pliers

1. To make the multiple shapes, draw three 6cm (2⅜in) diameter circles onto the paper. Cut out the circles, fold in half and cut along the folded line.

2. Fold each semicircle in half again so that you have six folded semicircles.

3. To assemble the shapes, place five of the semicircles side by side, then butt up against each other and glue the adjacent halves together. Add the sixth semicircle, gluing one half to the fifth semicircle and one half to the first to complete the shape. Press all the joined sides together firmly.

4. To add the wire hanger, thread a large and small bead onto an eye pin. Push the pin down through the decoration and thread another bead onto the end. Twist the end of the wire into a loop to keep the pin in place.

5. Make several of the decorations and thread onto a length of embroidery thread or thin wire to make a garland.

Tips and Tricks

Try joining six heart shapes cut from pastel shades of vellum, and hang upside down for a delicate teardrop garland.

Give leftover Christmas gift wrap a new lease of life by joining six circles to create baubles. Perfect for a New Year's party!

techniques ... basic tools

3D paper letters

Spell out the birthday boy's (or girl's) name in style. Using a simple font, each over-sized letter is cut from brightly-coloured card and decorated with bold stripes and dots to really make an impression.

you will need ...

- two A4 (US letter) sheets of lightweight card (per letter)
- A4 (US letter) sheets of paper, assorted colours
- small circle punch

1. Print out the name in your chosen typeface and enlarge on a photocopier to the size that you want. Use as a template to cut out each letter twice from lightweight card, using a craft knife to cut around curves for a really smooth finish. Put one set of letters aside and decorate the remaining set of letters. Cut strips of coloured paper and glue to the letter front in horizontal or diagonal stripes, trimming to fit. Punch small coloured circles and glue on randomly.

2. To join the two sets of letters together, make 'spacers' from the card off-cuts. Cut 6cm (2⅜in) wide strips of card, one for each upright section of the letter, making them slightly shorter so that they won't show when they are glued in place. Score and crease a 1cm (⅜in) border down each side of the strips.

3. Apply strips of narrow double-sided tape to the folded borders of the card spacers. Place the undecorated letter on a flat surface. Remove the backing from one spacer border strip and stick to the letter. Remove the backing from the second border strip; position the decorated letter over, and stick down, aligning the edges of the letters as closely as possible.

techniques ... basic tools

cocktail glasses

Jazz up your cocktail party with customized glasses, using bright summery colours and bead embellishments. Multi-surface gloss paints are designed to create a three-dimensional effect with a slightly raised surface that is ideal for adhering decorative accents to.

you will need ...

- two cocktail glasses
- multi-surface gloss paints: bright yellow, bright red, cinnamon, pink
- 0.5mm (size 5) gutta nib
- size 9 seed beads: red, pink, orange, yellow

1. Trace the outline of the large template onto tracing paper and cut out as a circle. Check that the shape fits inside your particular glass and adjust if required. Go over the outline with a fine black pen. Tape the template into a cone shape and secure inside the glass with masking tape. You are now ready to apply the glass paints.

2. The multi-surface paint comes in a container with a nozzle for ease of use, but for greater control when making the finer lines, a metal nozzle (like the ones used for silk painting) is used. Fit the gutta nib onto the tip of the orange gloss paint. Turn the glass upside down on a flat surface and draw the small loops out from the top of the stem. Turn the glass round to face you each time you draw a loop as the thickness of the stem distorts the pattern slightly.

3. Fit a nib on the yellow and pink gloss paints and draw the larger loops. Finally, draw fine straight lines in red between the petals and add a dot of red paint at the end of each line.

4. The drying time of the paint depends on the room temperature and the thickness of the line, and you need to add the beads before it begins to dry. Use a pin to lift the seed beads onto the paint. Space the beads along the length of each petal and put one at the end of each line. Add a few dots of orange paint and some orange beads to complete the design.

5. Trace the base template onto a piece of tracing paper and cut out to the size of your glass. Stick in place under the base. Stand the glass on the work surface and draw in the paint lines as before then decorate with seed beads.

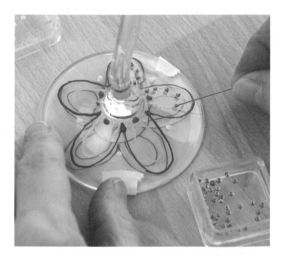

6. Leave the glass overnight to dry. To finish the design, squeeze a small quantity of pink gloss paint into a container, add a little red to darken and then paint the stem with a thin even coat. Leave overnight to dry again.

Tips and Tricks

Multi-surface paints are available in a wide range of colours and finishes, including metallic, pearl and crystal.

Try pastel pearl paint for a wedding or subtle metallic colours for Christmas.

Welcome your Christmas party guests with a line of sparkly baubles hung from various lengths along the windows of your house Decorate with a star motif and embellish with tiny beads and sequins.

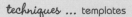

techniques ... templates

pink tiara

Who says you need diamonds to be queen of the ball? Make your own glamorous headgear for a fraction of the price. This finished tiara has been decorated with sequins and punched holes, but all sorts of other decorations would work just as well on this lightweight card, especially glitter!

you will need ...

- A2 (16½ x 23⅜in) sheet of pearlescent lilac lightweight card
- scraps of gold and purple lightweight card
- small gemstones

1. Use the tiara template to cut the outline from the lilac card, working carefully on the back of the card and using a scalpel.

3. Place the crown right-side up. Use an eyelet punch fitted with a small head attachment to make holes around the central section of the tiara; and an eyelet punch fitted with a medium head attachment to make holes along the centre of the band.

2. On the front of the tiara, score and crease around the curves where marked. Score a faint line along the centre of the crown band to make a guideline to punch along.

4. For the crown decorations cut a long, 6mm (¼in) wide strip of gold card. Concertina-fold the strip and glue it along the lower edge of the tiara band. Cut five circles from gold and purple card. Snip each one once from the edge to the centre, then overlap and glue the sides to make shallow cones. Glue along the crown band.

5. Cut a heart from purple card. Score and crease as marked. Attach to the top of the crown with an adhesive foam pad. Glue small gemstones around the central panel of the tiara. (Instead of gemstones, you could use holographic adhesive dots or punched silver dots.)

6. Place the tiara around the head and mark where the ends overlap. Glue or tape the ends of the tiara together.

Tips and Tricks

You can easily adapt the tiara to become an ice queen for a Christmas party. Use blue pearlescent card, draw on a swirly pattern with a silver metallic pen, and add some icy glitter sprinkles along the raised edges too.

To turn your man into your prince, make him a crown from gold card – an elegant scallop-edged fleur-de-lys panel design has been used here, and a red tissue paper dome fixed inside.

celebration bunting

Bunting brings a festive air to any occasion. While the red, white and blue of this flag garland makes it particularly suitable for Fourth of July celebrations, you can choose just about any colour combination you want. The flags are very easy to create – just cut them out and attach them to the bunting cord – making this an ideal last-minute project.

you will need ...

- 16 pieces of 40 x 20cm (15⅝ x 8in) medium-to heavy-weight cotton fabrics
- 4m (157in) of 4mm (³⁄₁₆in) cotton piping cord
- pinking shears

1. Use the flag template to cut 16 flags from your fabric selection — a variety of checks, stripes, plains and spots were used for this bunting. To make the double-sided flags, fold each piece of fabric with wrong sides facing, place the template on the fabric fold, and cut out with the pinking shears. Press.

2. The cotton piping cord measurement has been calculated as five flags to 1m (39½in) with a 4cm (1½in) gap between each flag. Allow 50cm (20in) at each end of the cord to tie the bunting. Open up the flag to the wrong side and place the cord on the fold line.

3. Close the flag. Pin at the bottom point, lining up the pinked edge, and then pin across the top, close to the cord (you should still be able to move the flags freely along the cord). Repeat for each flag, measuring 4cm (1½in) between each and then pin through the edge of the flag and cord to keep secure.

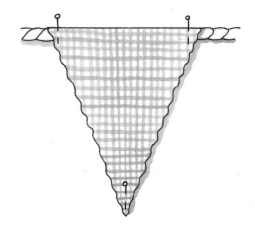

4. Starting at the top right-hand edge of the first flag, machine stitch through the cord and down the length of the flag to the bottom point 6mm (¼in) from the edge. With the needle in the down position, lift the foot, turn and sew up to the top left-hand edge.

5. Change to the zipper foot and alter the needle position to the farthest right. Then stitch as near to the cord edge as possible without sewing through the cord. Repeat on each flag and press.

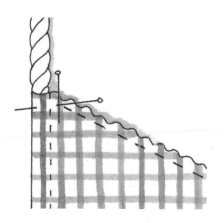

Tips and Tricks

A lighter-weight cotton would be suitable for indoor bunting but outdoor bunting requires a heavier-weight fabric to keep its shape in wet and windy weather.

Try orange fabrics and a pumpkin appliqué, or purple fabrics with black cat and bat motifs, for a Halloween party.

For a summer wedding make your flags from pretty white, pink and cream vintage linens strung on a length of lace ribbon.

techniques ... sewing techniques ... templates

sweet treats

cocktail cookies

Just what you need for a fun night with the girls! Instructions have been given for the zingy green cocktail here, but you can experiment with coloured sugarpaste to create your favourite tipple.

you will need ...

- cocktail glass-shaped cookies
- sugarpaste: white, red, deep green, pale yellow
- cocktail glass cookie cutters
- cutting wheel
- Dresden tool
- paste colours: green, yellow

1. First cover the cookies. Begin by rolling out white sugarpaste to a thickness of 3mm (⅛in) and cut out a glass shape. With a cutting wheel, make a 'V' cut at the base of the bowl of the glass and remove the top of the glass, leaving just the stem. Place the stem on the cookie.

2. Roll out green and white sugarpaste to a thickness of 3mm (⅛in) and cut into 2.5cm (1in) wide strips. Place the strips adjacent to each other and, with a finger, stroke one colour over the other to give a partially mixed appearance; flatten with a rolling pin. Using the cookie cutter and cutting wheel, cut out the striped paste to form the bowl of the glass and position on the cookie.

3. For the pineapple, thickly roll out the yellow paste, cut out a triangle and add texture by pressing the Dresden tool deeply into it. Using the cookie cutter, cut the shape to fit the glass and attach to the cookie. Add a red paste cherry.

4. Mix the green and yellow paste colours separately with cooled boiled water. Paint green horizontal lines over the green section of the glass and yellow over the pineapple.

techniques ... basic tools ... sugarcraft techniques ... recipes

swirl cupcakes

This attractive rose design is perfect for an informal wedding reception, especially if the frosting is coloured to match the bride's theme. They are quick and easy to make – ideal if large quantities are required.

you will need ...

- buttercream of your choice
- pink food colouring
- piping bag and large star piping tip
- cupcakes

1. Colour half the batch of buttercream with the pink food colouring, then colour a small amount of this deep pink.

2. Place the large star tube into a large piping bag. Put the pink buttercream in one side of your piping bag, a little deep pink in the centre, and then fill the other side of the bag with the uncoloured buttercream – this will give you a piped marbled effect.

3. Holding the bag vertically, start piping at the centre of the cupcake. Apply pressure to the bag, then move the tip to the edge of the cake and go around the centre in a clockwise direction. Release the pressure and remove the piping bag when you have completed the circle.

streamers cake

It's often the traditional trappings of a good old-fashioned celebration that best capture the party spirit. This dramatic birthday cake rejoices in those retro party-time favourites – streamers, stars and balloons – in unashamedly bright colours. These are beautifully contrasted with the deep chocolate icing, although a plain white icing would also work well.

you will need ...

- 13cm (5in) and one 20cm (8in) deep round cake
- buttercream
- 28cm (11in) round cake board
- 2kg (4½lb) chocolate-flavoured sugarpaste for covering
- 50g (1¾oz) chocolate-flavoured sugarpaste for the stars
- three hollow dowels

- brown satin ribbon 1.5cm (⅝in) wide
- 1.5ml (¼ teaspoon) CMC
- edible glue
- small star plunger cutter
- 350g (12oz) white flower paste
- food colourings: pink, yellow, blue, green, purple, orange
- small metal star cutter

1. Fill the cakes with buttercream. Cover the cakes and ice the cake board with chocolate-flavoured sugarpaste.

2. Start by dowelling the bottom tier of the cake and assemble the two tiers on the iced cake board. Wrap the ribbon around the base of each tier and the cake board, and secure with double-sided tape.

3. Knead the CMC into the chocolate-flavoured sugarpaste to make it stiffer and roll it out thinly with a small non-stick rolling pin on a small non-stick board set over a non-slip mat. Cut small stars using the small plunger cutter. Stick them onto the cake in a random fashion around the tops of each tier with a small amount of edible glue.

4. Divide the white flower paste into six pieces and colour each one with a different food colouring, kneading the icing thoroughly. Keep the colours as bright as possible.

5. To make the streamers, roll out a small amount of one of the flower paste colours into a strip about 20cm (8in) long. Cut an even, narrow strip about 5mm (³⁄₁₆in) thick from the paste and twist it around a thin plastic dowel. Pinch the two ends together so that they come to a point, and set aside to stiffen a little.

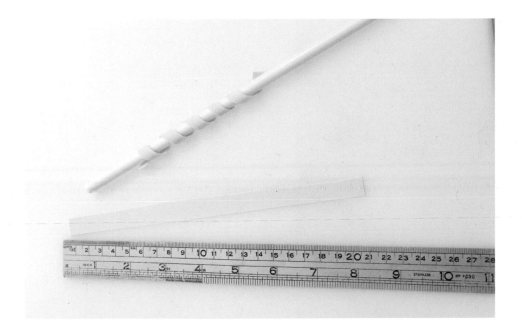

6. Mark six points around the bottom tier, an equal distance apart, and four points on the top tier – you can simply judge this by sight. Before the streamer is completely dry, stick it to the cake between two points using edible glue. Repeat with all the colours until you have streamers around both the top and bottom tiers.

7. Roll out more narrow strips for the hanging streamers. Curl up one end and wrap around the dowel to stiffen before sticking on the cake. Roll more strips, 7.5cm (3in) long, for the bows and fold in the two ends, pinching in the centre to join. Cut out ten brown and ten coloured stars with the small metal cutter. Stick a brown star to each bow. Then stick a coloured star on top to match the hanging streamer so that its points are positioned between the points of the brown star.

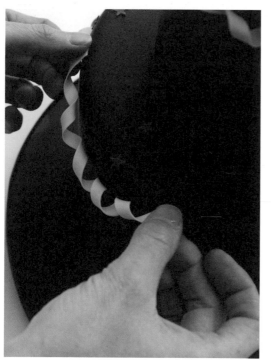

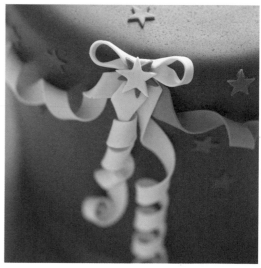

Tips and Tricks

Be inspired by the cake to decorate the party area; use plenty of streamers and balloons in neon colours!

The Streamer Cake can be adapted to make a stunning wedding cake. Cover the cakes with white sugarpaste, hang white streamers all around the edges, and replace the stars with pink and red hearts.

For a christening cake, use blue streamers and stars for a boy and pink for a girl.

For an extra treat, decorate chocolate cupcakes with delicious chocolate buttercream and neon-coloured sugarpaste stars.

techniques ... sugarcraft techniques ... recipes ... covering a round cake ... icing cake boards ... assembling tiered cakes

streamers cake 47

present cookies

What better birthday gift could there be than a box of present cookies? They are made using a gift-shaped cutter and decorated with coloured sugarpaste. Alternatively, they would make a wonderful wedding reception favour.

you will need ...

- gift-shaped cookies
- sugarpaste: dark brown, mid brown, pink, deep pink, violet, white
- gift-shaped cookie cutter
- circle cutters: 4.5cm (1¾in), 3.5cm (1⅜in), 2.5cm (1in)
- piping tubes no. 4, 16, 18

1. First cover the cookies. Roll out dark brown sugarpaste to a thickness of 3mm (⅛in) and cut out a gift shape. Cut away the top section and attach the remainder to the cookie.

2. Thinly roll out sugarpaste in each colour for creating the concentric circles and cover with plastic wrap to prevent drying.

3. Using a 4.5cm (1¾in) circle cutter, cut a circle from the deep pink paste. Take the 3.5cm (1⅜in) circle cutter and centrally remove a circle from the larger circle. Replace this circle with a mid brown one and blend the join

between the two circles by rubbing a finger over the pastes to smooth out any gaps. Repeat with the 2.5cm (1in) circle and replace with a coffee coloured circle. Continue removing and replacing circles of different colours using the piping tubes as circle cutters. Attach to the cookie and trim the edges as necessary. Continue to decorate with a selection of concentric circle motifs in different sizes and colours, referring to the finished photo for inspiration.

4. Roll balls of deep pink paste to decorate the top of the gift and attach in place.

smiley lollipops

These cheerful white chocolate lollipops decorated with red, white and blue ribbons make a great treat for your Fourth of July celebrations. Arrange a few lollipops in a glass or a small vase to create a fun table centrepiece.

you will need (for four giant lollipops) ...

- 600g (1lb 5oz) white couverture chocolate
- disposable piping bag
- lollipop mould
- four lollipop sticks
- 40g (1½oz) dark chocolate paste
- sugar gun
- narrow ribbon: red, white, blue

1. Temper the white couverture chocolate and use a disposable piping bag to pipe it into a lollipop mould that has been gently warmed with a dry heat.

2. Place the lollipop stick into the tempered chocolate and roll it to coat it evenly. Tap the mould gently onto the work surface to disperse any air bubbles. Leave in the fridge to set for approx. 20 minutes, then remove from the mould.

3. Knead the dark chocolate paste for a few seconds until it becomes tacky and place it into the sugar gun with the smallest nozzle in place. Squeeze the sugar gun until it makes a long string of chocolate paste to form the smile and use a paintbrush to guide the paste into place. The paste should stick to the lollipop.

4. Roll two tiny balls of paste to form the eyes and press onto the lollipop. Tie the ribbons around the lollipop stick.

techniques ... basic tools ... sugarcraft techniques ... tempering chocolate

hedgehog cake

There is no better centrepiece to a party table than a novelty cake, and this is one of the best. Although it looks quite complicated, it is actually quite simple to make. Chocolate cake is simply carved to shape and then partially covered with sugarpaste. The delicious prickles are made from flaked chocolate, and will prove irresistible for chocolate lovers.

you will need ...

- 25.5 x 20cm (10 x 8in) rectangular chocolate cake
- two quantities of chocolate buttercream
- paste colours: golden brown, dark brown
- 30cm (12in) round cake board
- 800g (1¾lb) white sugarpaste
- 1.5ml (¼ teaspoon) CMC
- 200g (7oz) brown sugarpaste

- 48 flaked chocolate bars
- 15g (½oz) white modelling paste
- 25g (1oz) black modelling paste
- oval cutters: 4.5cm (1¾in), 2.8cm (1³⁄₃₂in), 2.3cm (1⁵⁄₁₆in)
- golden-brown ribbon
- edible glue

1. Level the cake to a height of 6.5cm (2½in), then cut it in half to give two 13 x 20cm (5 x 8in) rectangles. Spread buttercream over the top of one cake and stack the second on top. Make outline and profile templates from greaseproof paper and place the outline template on top of the stacked cake. With a large knife, cut vertically around the template.

2. Using glass-headed dressmakers' pins to secure, place the profile template onto one side of the cake. Holding the knife horizontally, cut away the cake along the outline of the template. Put the cake in the freezer and leave overnight

3. Now move on to cover the board. Using the golden-brown paste colour, colour the white sugarpaste five shades of golden brown. Break the coloured paste into small pieces and scatter them over your work surface to mix up the colours. Gather the scattered pieces together into a ball and briefly knead together. Cut across the ball to reveal the marbled pattern inside. Place the two halves next to one another and then roll the paste out to a 5mm (³⁄₁₆in) thickness. Ice the board with the marbled paste. Use double-sided tape to attach the ribbon around the sides of the board.

4. To make golden brown modelling paste for working the facial details later, take 50g (2oz) of golden-brown sugarpaste trimmings and knead in the CMC. Leave to mature overnight.

5. Remove the cake from the freezer. Insert cocktail sticks in a central line over the top of the cake. To create the curved appearance, cut from the central line of cocktail sticks to the horizontal buttercream line around the sides, where the two sections of cake meet, using a curved cut. Then curve all the cut edges of the snout to shape. Finally, remove a wedge of cake from below the horizontal line all the way around the base. Cut away small pieces of cake at a time to avoid removing too much.

6. Place the cake on waxed paper and spread a thin layer of buttercream over the face area. Knead the brown sugarpaste until warm then roll out to a thickness of 5mm (³⁄₁₆in) and place over

the buttercream area of cake. Ease in the fullness of paste around the sides of the cake and bring the excess together under the snout. Cut away the excess paste using a small pair of scissors.

7. Smooth the paste firstly with a smoother and then use the heat of your hand to create an even surface. Cut away the excess paste at the base with a palette knife and then remove the excess from around the face.

8. Now add the spines. Cover the front half of the body with a thick layer of buttercream. Place the bars of flaked chocolate on a chopping board and use a sharp knife to cut in half; then split each half lengthways into three or four sections. You may find it easier to chill the chocolate bars in the fridge before splitting. Insert a row of spines into the cake centrally from one side to the other by pushing the spines gently in until they are held securely.

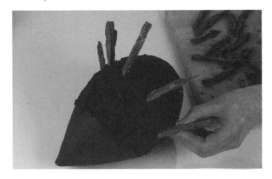

9. Next, insert a row of spines from the spine in the centre of the back to the face, decreasing the size and changing the angle as the spines come down towards the face. Now fill the marker spines with spines of the appropriate size, referring to the finished cake photo for guidance.

10. Carefully transfer the cake to the covered cake board. Cover the remaining cake with a thick layer of buttercream and insert the flaked chocolate as before. To prevent the spines from falling at the back before the buttercream sets, support them as necessary with small pieces of foam. Leave to set.

11. The facial details are cut from thinly rolled out modelling paste, using a set of oval cutters to make the distinctive eyes that give the hedgehog such character. Cut two 4.5cm (1¾in) ovals from white paste, two 3cm (1⅛in) from golden-brown paste and two 2.3cm (¹⁵/₁₆in) from black paste. Place the golden-brown and black ovals at one end of the larger white ovals, and cut away the excess with the largest oval cutter. Shape the lower edge of the white of the eye with a cutting wheel. Cut a small white triangle and add to the top of each eye for a highlight. Attach in place on the cake using edible glue to secure.

12. To make the whiskers and eyelashes, roll out black modelling paste to a thickness of 1.5mm (¹⁄₁₆in). Take the cutting wheel and run it backwards and forwards through the paste to create long, thin triangles. Cut across the base of the triangles and arrange three on either side of the snout, secure in place with edible glue and support with pins until dry. Attach two smaller triangles to the corner of each eye and turn the ends up slightly to curve.

13. To make the nose, roll a small amount of golden-brown sugarpaste into a ball and anchor to the tip of the snout with a small length of uncooked spaghetti.

Tips and Tricks

Make your guests individual spiky cakes. Bake half-ball-shaped mini-cakes using a mini-ball pan and cover with dark brown chocolate buttercream. To make the head, roll brown sugarpaste into a ball, then a cone; hollow out the wider end with your thumb and stick to the cake. Break flavoured chocolate sticks into pieces; insert into the cake and leave to dry. Add a face, this time using small cutters.

animal cupcakes

Three sweet little animal designs decorate these delicious cupcakes. They are easy to make by imaginatively combining shapes cut from sugarpaste and they are a fun and colourful addition to any children's party.

you will need ...

- peach sugarpaste
- mini embossers
- circle cutter
- cupcakes
- buttercream
- modelling paste: green, blue, deep pink, black, white
- selection of small shape cutters

1. Knead the sugarpaste until warm, then roll it out to a thickness of 5mm (³⁄₁₆in). Take one or more of the small embossers and press repeatedly into the sugarpaste to create textured patterns on it. Cut out circles from the textured sugarpaste using a circle cutter that fits the top of your cupcakes. Brush the cakes with a thin layer of buttercream to help the sugarpaste circles stick on. Use a palette knife to carefully lift a circle onto each cake.

2. Separately, roll out the different colours of modelling paste to a thickness of 1.5mm (¹⁄₁₆in) and texture some or all with the mini embossers.

3. Use the shape cutters (oval, heart, paisley, teardrop, flower) to cut out a selection of shapes and use to create the cute animal designs. The dog is made with a heart for its body, an oval for its head and two paisleys for its ears. The cat has a paisley for its body and oval for its head. The rabbit is made from ovals and teardrops. Attach the designs to the top of the cakes using a small paintbrush and a little water. Add a flower or two to complete.

techniques ... basic tools ... sugarcraft techniques ... recipes

58 animal cupcakes

cards and gifts

balloons pop-up card

Pop-ups bring a wealth of 3D fun to a card design and they are always a big hit with children. You can so easily turn a single fold card into a great little pop-up design with this simple technique. Stamped balloons cut out and mounted on wire appear to be popping out of the gift as the card is opened. The surprise is only revealed when the card is opened. To keep the secret for as long as possible, decorate the front of the card with a balloon-patterned paper.

you will need ...

- printed paper: numbers, stripe
- 15 x 10cm (6 x 4in) white single fold card
- very narrow pink ribbon
- balloons rubber stamp
- black inkpad
- lightweight card: yellow, blue, red
- thin silver wire
- wire cutters

1. Fold the numbers paper in half and measuring 6cm (2⅜in) up from the bottom make a 6cm (2⅜in) horizontal slit across the fold line. Fold the paper and crease at the left and right side where the slit ends. This will make a tab that pops up once the card is open.

2. Cut slits 4.5cm (1¾in) and 5.5cm (2¼in) down from the top of the numbers paper making the slits about 4.5cm (1¾in) wide; this will make a tab for the balloons.

3. Stick the numbers paper onto the single fold card taking care to keep the pop-up parts free of glue. Glue a square of stripe paper onto the lower pop-up box and decorate with ribbon tied in a bow.

4. Stamp the balloon image onto the yellow, red and blue card. Cut the balloons out and layer one red and one blue balloon onto the yellow balloons with adhesive foam pads.

5. Cut 6cm (2⅜in) lengths of wire and loosely wrap around a cocktail stick, remove from the stick and secure to the reverse of the balloons with adhesive foam pads. Fix the balloons to the slits on the inside of the card.

Tips and Tricks

Make matching place name cards for the party table. Stamp the balloons onto the centre of the card before cutting around the top and folding in half. This is a great way to achieve a pop-up effect without having to cut slits or make tabs!

beaded gift bags

These small bead-fringed gift bags are ideal when giving jewellery. They are made from wide wire-edged ribbon so there are no awkward seams to finish. Simply wrap the present in toning tissue paper and pop it inside the bag. Attach a few bead strands to a short length of craft wire and secure around the neck of the gift bag before tying the ribbon bow.

you will need (for the pink bag) ...

- pink wire-edged sheer ribbon 7cm (2¾in) wide x 38cm (15in)

- pink wire-edged sheer ribbon 2.5cm (1in) wide x 50cm (20in)

- sewing thread: pink, lime green

- 2g size 11 seed beads: lime, bright green

- 20 green 5mm crystal beads

- 13 green 10mm teardrop beads

- size 10 beading needle

- 0.5mm (25swg) silver-plated craft wire

1. Fold the wider sheer ribbon in half and then fold over the ends to the inside to make a 12cm (4¾in) bag shape. Trim the folded ends to 4cm (1½in). Sew the side seams with matching thread beginning 3cm (1⅛in) from the top edge. Backstitch a few stitches at each end of the seam to secure the threads and then trim neatly.

2. To begin the bead fringe, cut eight 30cm (12in) lengths of lime green sewing thread. Fold a length in half and feed the cut ends into the beading needle. Sew a tiny stitch into the corner of the bag and then take the needle through the loop and pull taut. Add a double thread in the same way at 1cm (⅜in) gaps and into the other corner. Leave the needle on the last pair of threads.

3. Using the threaded needle, pick up seven seed beads, alternating between the lime and the bright green, then pick up a crystal, a further six seed beads and another crystal. Leave the pair of thread ends lying.

4. Thread the beading needle with one of the threads from the next pair. Pick up seven seed beads, alternating between the lime and the bright green, and then take the needle through the first crystal on the adjacent bead strand. Add a further six seed beads and another crystal. Leave the thread end lying.

5. Thread the beading needle onto the other single thread and pick up seven seed beads, a crystal, seven seed beads and feed the needle through the last crystal on the adjacent bead strand. Leave the thread lying.

6. Repeat steps 4 and 5 to bead each pair of threads across the bottom of the bag. Finish the bead fringing by threading the final pair of threads at the other corner onto a needle and picking up the same sequence of beads as the opposite corner.

7. On each pair of threads left lying along the bottom of the fringing pick up a seed bead and a teardrop bead.

8. Feed the needle back through the seed bead and then up through the bead strand. Work a half hitch knot on either side of the top crystal and then feed the thread through a few more seed beads before trimming the end.

9. Cut a 10cm (4in) length of wire. Attach a long double length of thread onto the wire by feeding the needle through the loop and pulling taut. Pick up the beads listed in step 3 to make a single-beaded strand.

10. Take the needle back through the seed beads and crystals. Work a half hitch over the wire and then make another similar strand a slightly different length. Make five bead strands in all and secure the thread.

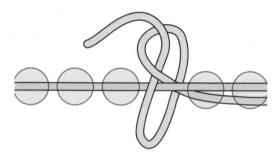

11. Fill the gift bag, secure with the beaded wire and then tie the narrow sheer ribbon in a bow. Trim the ends of the ribbon neatly to finish.

Tips and Tricks

You can make your beaded gift bags as unique as the gifts inside simply by changing the bead colour and pattern.

For the white bag, short bugles and bright pink pearls add a contrast of textures to this simple looped fringe. Begin by securing the thread at one side and make the small loops first. Work back across adding the longer loops, then attach a few bead loops to the neck of the gift bag.

For the green bag, larger beads are only added at the end of alternate strands of a plain bead fringe with the strands in between left slightly shorter so that the fringe has weight but still hangs straight. Repeat bead patterns on alternate strands to coordinate the design.

handbag gift bag

What could be more appealing to a style-loving girl than a gift bag modelled on the chic designer handbags so often seen on the catwalk? This gift bag is made by layering different papers and stitching them together on the sewing machine. It has a generous gusset to accommodate bulky presents and a simple fastening to keep the gifts safely secured inside. The front pocket provides the perfect hiding place for a small surprise gift or a message written on a coordinating tag.

you will need ...

- A3 (12 x 16½in) sheet of brown paper
- A2 (16½ x 23⅜in) sheet of green paper
- A4 (US letter) sheet of pink patterned paper
- scraps of plain and patterned papers
- A3 (12 x 16½in) sheet of blue patterned paper
- dark brown thread
- medium-gauge wire
- punches: daisy, single-hole

1. Cut a handbag front from brown paper and a back from green paper. Cut a front panel from pink patterned paper and glue it in place on the bag front. Cut a 1cm (⅜in) wide strip of orange paper to fit along the bottom edge of the front panel. Glue the paper strip in place and then overstitch on the sewing machine. Cut a pocket from green paper and the flower petals and flower centre from patterned papers. Glue the flower to the pocket, then overstitch. Stitch the pocket to the bag front.

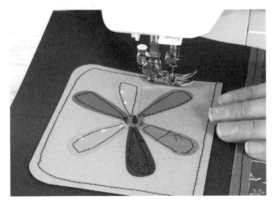

2. Cut a top and side border from blue patterned paper. Glue the strips to the bag front. Using a single-hole punch, punch a hole at the top of the bag front and back at either side for the handles.

3. Cut a 10 x 80cm (4 x 31½in) green paper strip. Score and crease a 1cm (⅜in) wide border down each side. Snip along the borders, then curve and glue around the inside edges of the bag front and back. Trim the excess flush with the bag top.

4. To make the bag fastening cut a green paper strap. Punch a daisy from brown paper, and glue onto an orange paper circle. Overstitch around the edge of the strap. Glue the circle to the rounded end of the strap. Attach the other strap end to the bag with double-sided tape.

5. To make the handles curve two 50cm (20in) lengths of wire into handle shapes. Punch about 40 flowers and masses of dots from scraps of plain and patterned papers; using a sharp needle, thread these onto the handles, interspersing the flowers with equal blocks of dots. Thread the ends of the handles through the holes in the bag front and back, and form into small loops. Twist the free ends of the wire around the loops to close.

Tips and Tricks

You can create different handbag shapes, such as a square or circular bag, and if you don't have a sewing machine, you could simply draw on stitches with a fine-nib pen.

Experiment with various types of paper, such as a highly textured or stitched paper, or offcuts of flocked wallpaper.

techniques ... papercraft techniques ... stitching paper ... templates

mirrored gift boxes

These bright citrus-coloured gift boxes make eye-catching containers for awkward to wrap presents. They are quickly created using ready-made, lidded cardboard boxes covered with felt, then edged with embroidery stitching and decorated with ornately framed shisha mirrors. Further bead embellishments and sparkling sequins add to the exotic flavour.

you will need (for the large orange box) ...

- cardboard box with lid 9cm (3½in) tall and 6.5cm (2½in) in diameter
- 25.5cm (10in) square of orange felt
- pink stranded cotton (floss)
- 10 gold shisha mirrors with frames
- pink seed beads
- 10 pink flower sequins
- narrow pink ribbon
- gold nail-head sequins

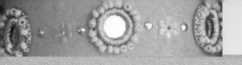

1. Measure the circumference of the base of the box and cut a strip of double-sided tape to the same length, allowing an overlap of 1.3cm (½in). Peel away the backing from one side of the tape and carefully stick it around the box base, butting up to the rim and overlapping at the join. Cut another strip the same length and trim the width as necessary, then lay it over the remaining area of the box base.

2. Cut a piece of felt 2cm (¾in) wider than the overall width of the box base and 2cm (¾in) longer than the overall length. Remove the remaining backing from the tape and carefully lay the felt onto the box base, butting one long edge of the felt up to the rim.

3. Mark and trim the end of the felt to achieve an exact, neat join, then run over the surface of the felt with your fingers to create a smooth finish. Using small embroidery scissors, cut away the excess around the bottom edge of the box. Cover the side of the box lid in the same way.

4. Place the lid, top down, on the felt and draw around it with a fade-away marker. Removing the backing, cover the back of the felt circle with strips of double-sided tape, overlapping the circle slightly. Use embroidery scissors to cut out the circle, then peel away the remaining backing and stick the felt onto the lid, smoothing over the surface as in step 3. Cover the bottom of the box base in the same way.

5. Using three strands of stranded cotton (floss), sew a row of large, even blanket stitches around the top edge and rim of the felt-covered lid.

6. Sew about 10 seed beads around the edge of the shisha mirrors; glue the decorated shisha mirrors around the centre of the box side spacing them equally. Stick on pink sequins in between the mirrors.

7. Make a small slit at the centre of the lid and thread through a narrow ribbon loop. Tie the ribbon ends in a knot and trim the excess. Decorate the side of the lid by gluing on a series of evenly spaced nail-head sequins.

Tips and Tricks

Cardboard boxes, such as those used for this project, are available in all different sizes. Choose the one that is most suitable for the gift you have bought.

To continue the exotic Eastern theme, decorate the party table mats and napkins with coordinating shisha mirror and sequin embellishments.

techniques ... sewing techniques ... blanket stitch ... attaching seed beads and sequins

gift token card

This greetings card is designed to hold a music token attached to an actual size, mirror card CD. The CD slots comfortably into a square envelope transformed into a groovy bag for a music-loving friend. The envelope has a button and string fastening to keep the token safe and secure inside. For a young, fun look, vibrant, clashing colours and a retro-style stamp have been used, but you can easily adapt the paper choices to match your friend's tastes.

you will need ...

- A4 (US letter) sheet thick white card
- 15cm (6in) square mirror card
- scraps of thin silver and pink card
- 14cm (5½in) square pink envelope
- spotted paper: green, blue
- flower stamp and red inkpad
- punches: heart, daisy
- pink metallic eyelets
- wavy edge scissors
- pink lurex cord

1. Lay the pink envelope face down and stamp the flower design onto the flap. Leave to dry for a few minutes. Stamp the flower design onto the green spotted paper, and cut out two small circles from it.

2. Carefully open out the envelope, and lay it flat. On the right side of the envelope, attach the daisy circles to the top and bottom flaps with eyelets. Glue the envelope together again.

3. Cut five 1cm (⅜in) strips of green spotted paper. Cut a wavy edge on three of the strips. Glue two wavy strips to the underside of the flap so that the decorative edge shows on the front, the third wavy strip across the bottom, and the other two strips down the sides.

4. Using the tag template, cut a tag from flower-stamped pink card. Decorate the sides and bottom edges with more strips of green spotted paper trimmed with wavy edge scissors. Punch two hearts from the thin silver card. Punch a hole in one and attach it to the top of the tag with an eyelet.

5. Punch two daisies from green paper. Glue them in the centre of the red stamped flowers, one on the envelope flap and one on the tag.

6. Cut a 1cm (⅜in) wide, 30cm (12in) long strip of green spotted paper and fold it diagonally in two places to make a handle shape. Glue to the back of the envelope bag. Fold the white card in half and cover the front with blue spotted paper. Glue the envelope bag to the card, leaving the handle free.

7. Draw around a CD onto the mirror card and cut out. Attach the token to the back of the card CD and push it into the envelope. Cut a length of pink lurex cord, tie it to the tag through the eyelet hole and tie the tag to the handle. Punch a hole in the second silver heart. Wrap lurex cord around the two daisy circles to close the bag, and tie on the heart.

Tips and Tricks

For a friend that loves to buy clothes, present your gift token in a real pocket, cut from an old pair or jeans and stuck onto a covered card blank using a strong adhesive. Just make sure that the pocket is big enough for the token!

beaded star cards

What better way to announce your Christmas party than with these gorgeous invitation cards? They are so quick and easy to make and the contemporary designs really stand out. Choose printed papers in bright raspberry reds or zingy lime greens and complete with pretty polka-dot ribbon. Sisal shapes have a wonderful rough texture that contrasts with the shiny beads and wire.

you will need ...

- A4 (US letter) off-white card
- stripe paper
- polka-dot ribbon, 2cm (¾in) wide
- 0.4mm (27swg) silver-plated wire
- size 11 red seed beads
- star beads: red, pink, clear
- mixed beads: red, clear
- round-nosed pliers
- two sisal stars
- ric-rac braid
- polka-dot brad

1. Cut an 18 x 13cm (7 x 5in) piece of card and score across the middle; fold in half to make a landscape card. Cut a piece of stripe paper to fit the front and tear down one long side about 2.5cm (1in) from the edge. Stick the paper onto the front of the card so that the long straight side is across the bottom edge. Stick a length of polka-dot ribbon across the paper and trim neatly.

2. Cut a 40cm (15⅝in) length of silver-plated wire and make a loop at one end to stop the beads falling off. * Pick up a red seed bead, a larger bead and another red seed bead; then pick up a star bead. Repeat from *, changing the colour of the star bead from red, to pink and then clear, until there are about seven star beads on the wire.

3. Wind the wire around a pair of round-nosed pliers to make a loop near the plain end. Bring the first three beads down to the loop and then make a second loop at the other side of the beads. Bring a star bead down the wire and make a loop at the other side. Continue making loops to one side or the other to space the beads along the length of the wire. Move some of the seed beads into the loops.

4. Attach the sisal star to the top left of the front of the card using a glue dot. Arrange the beaded wire across the card and bend to make an attractive arrangement. Use glue dots behind some of the star beads to attach the beaded wire. Attach a few single star beads on the right-hand side.

5. To make a tag, cut a 6 x 10.5cm (2¾ x 4⅛in) piece of card. Stick stripe paper and a sisal star on the front. Wrap wire around the tag, adding beads across the front. Stick a small piece of ribbon to the centre top and trim at an angle. Finish with ric-rac braid and a large polka-dot brad.

Tips and Tricks

To make the sparkling snowflake card, take a 21 x 16.5cm (8¼ x 6½in) piece of off-white card, score across the middle and fold in half. Cut a piece of striped paper to fit half the card and stick on the front. Tear a piece of green vellum and stick next to the striped paper. Cover the join with polka-dot ribbon and attach the snowflake sisal shape. Finish by attaching a green bead and wire decoration.

cupcake boxes

Cupcakes are all the rage, and these pretty paper sculpted versions make an unusual card for a Mother's Day celebration. Made from pastel-coloured papers, they look stunning en masse. Alternatively, a single cupcake looks just as good presented in its own colour-coordinated gift box (for instruction on making a baker's-style lidded box, see the Techniques section). Each cake hides a secret; lift the cone lid by its flower handle to reveal a little message, an invitation or a special thought.

you will need ...

- medium-weight paper in pastel shades: pink, orange, blue, yellow
- decorative scissors: scallop edge, zigzag edge
- pastel-coloured crimped card
- small label

1. Cut a cupcake base from pink paper. Score and crease around the inner circle where marked on the template. Snip at evenly spaced intervals around the base, from the outer edge to the inner scored circle, to make tabs. Fold the tabs under.

2. Cut a 1.5 x 22cm (⅝ x 8⅝in) strip of orange paper. Gently curl by pulling it over the closed blades of a pair of scissors. Cut along one long edge with the scallop edge scissors. Stick a length of narrow double-sided tape to the wrong side of the strip, then wrap the strip around the base covering the tabs.

3. Cut a cupcake top from blue paper. Snip from the edge to the centre where marked, then overlap the cut edges to make a cone that sits perfectly on the base. Place the cone unglued inside the base and overlap the edges until you achieve a perfect fit. Stick the overlapped edges together with double-sided tape.

4. To make the flower, use a pair of compasses to draw a 6cm (2⅜in) circle onto yellow paper and cut out. Fold the paper in half, then into quarters and finally into eighths. Using a pencil, draw a half petal adjoining each of the two folded edges. Carefully snip around the pencil lines, taking care not to cut through the folded edges. Unfold the paper to reveal a flower. Curl each petal in turn by pulling it over the closed blades of your scissors.

5. Cut a 2cm (¾in) wide strip of orange paper to make the stamens. Draw a faint line 6mm (¼in) from one long edge. Snip along the strip, making very narrow cuts, up to the pencil line. Tightly roll the strip and stick the ends together with double-sided tape. Fan out the stamens, then glue to the centre of the flower.

6. Cut a paper case from crimped card. Trim the upper edge with zigzag scissors. Tape the short edges together to measure approx. 8cm (3⅛in) across. Run a thin line of PVA (white) glue around the lower edge of the cake base. Place the cake gently in the case and make sure that it sits straight. Leave to dry. Write a message on a small label and place inside the cake.

Tips and Tricks

If you're short on time, you could use real cake cases, instead of crimped card.

For wedding reception favours, make the cakes from white paper with silver cases and scatter the tops with pink paper rosebuds.

For Easter treats, make cheeky Easter Bunny cupcakes to conceal a nest of delicious chocolate eggs.

techniques … papercraft techniques … making a lidded box … templates

techniques...

basic tools

Each project in the book has its own You Will Need list, detailing the specific materials and equipment required to make it. However, you will also need some general supplies, as listed below.

Sewing Tools

- fabric markers and pencils
- needles, pins and safety pins
- scissors (fabric and embroidery)
- tape measure
- sewing and embroidery threads
- sewing machine
- iron
- fusible web
- pressing cloth

Wirework/Beading Tools

- round-nose and long-nose pliers
- wire cutters
- beading needle

Sugarcraft Tools

- non-stick board with non-slip mat
- large and small non-stick rolling pin
- large and small sharp knife (for cutting/shaping icing)
- large serrated knife (for carving/sculpting cakes)
- palette knife (for applying buttercream)
- metal ruler
- greaseproof (wax) paper
- clingfilm (plastic wrap)
- 5mm (3/16in) spacers
- smoother (for smoothing icing)
- pastry brush
- Dresden tool (to create markings on paste)
- cutting wheel
- edible pen

Papercraft Tools

- craft knife, metal ruler and cutting mat
- tracing paper
- pair of compasses
- circle punches in small and medium
- bone folder (optional)
- double-sided tape and adhesive foam pads
- PVA (white) glue and glue dots
- eyelet punch and hammer

Other Tools

- masking tape
- paintbrush
- cocktail sticks (toothpicks)

sewing techniques

The techniques needed for creating the fabric projects in the book are given in this section. Some of these techniques may also be needed for the other projects.

Preparing fabric

Prepare your fabrics by pre-washing them before use in mild detergent to check that the colours do not run and to allow for any shrinkage that might occur. Pre-wash cotton lining or interfacings too. For delicate fabrics where washing is best avoided, such as silk and wool, gently tighten the fibres and help prevent shrinkage by hovering a steam iron 3–4cm (1¼ –1¾in) above the cloth.

Cutting fabric

It is important when cutting out to have a clean, large flat surface to work on and to always cut away from yourself.

If using fabric shears, ensure that they are sharp. To cut accurately, position your fabric to the left of the shears (or to the right if you are left-handed) and follow the edge of the pattern line, taking long strokes for straight edges and shorter strokes for curved areas.

Marking fabrics

There are many ways to mark designs on to fabrics before stitching; two are described here.

Using a fade-away pen

Any marks made with a fade-away pen will disappear in time (air-soluble) or with a little water (water-soluble). Use the pen to draw the line you want to follow with stitching. Once stitched, dab a little water on to remove water-soluble marks.

Using a fabric pencil or tailor's chalk

Any marks made with a fabric pencil or tailors' chalk will rub off when no longer needed. Draw the line or pattern with the pencil and take care not to rub it out as you stitch. Once the stitching is complete, rub the pencil marks to remove.

Sewing by hand

The projects in this book use a variety of hand stitches for functional and decorative work. When sewing by hand choose a needle that matches the thickness of the thread you are using, so the thread passes easily through the fabric. All stitches can be started with a knot on the back of the work and finished off neatly at the back, usually with some tiny backstitches.

Backstitch

Backstitch is often worked on its own for lettering or to add detail and can be worked to follow a design line.

Bring the needle and thread up to the front of the work and take a backward stitch, taking the needle and thread through to the back. Bring the needle up to the front again, a little way ahead of the first stitch, and back down into the point where the first stitch began. Repeat along the line to be stitched.

Blanket stitch

This stitch can be used to create a decorative edging, especially around appliqué motifs.

Working from left to right (or the opposite direction if left-handed), bring the needle and thread up from the back of the fabric to the front, a little way in from the edge, the distance depending on the size of stitches you want. Leave the loose thread running down over the edge or at right angles to it. Take the threaded end over the loose end and insert the needle a little way along, the same distance from the edge as before. Pass the needle through the loop of thread and pull up the thread so it fits snugly along the edge. Repeat along the edge to be stitched.

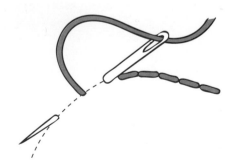

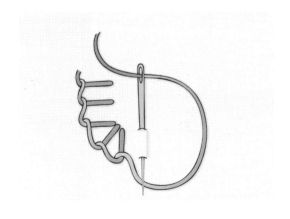

Slipstitch

This stitch is used for hems, to close gaps in seams, to attach pockets and so on – anywhere you do not want the stitches to show too much.

Work small, neat stitches in a thread that matches the fabric colour, so that the stitches are almost invisible. Work from right to left (if right-handed), picking up a tiny piece of the fabric from one seam edge with the needle. Insert the needle into the other seam fold, moving it along inside the fold about 3mm (⅛in). Push the needle out into the seam again and repeat.

Attaching seed beads and sequins

Beads and sequins are great for adding extra sparkle to your party projects as can be seen on the Mirrored Gift Boxes.

When sewing on sequins, bring the needle and thread up through the centre of the sequin and sew in place before finishing off by threading the needle back through the centre of the sequin again. Secure the thread with a knot before and after the sequin has been worked.

Sew on seed beads with a double length of thread, knotted before and after they are worked to ensure that they don't come off.

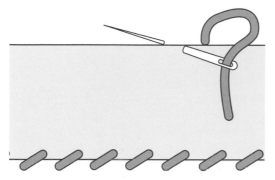

Sewing by machine

A sewing machine produces a consistent and strong stitch and will allow you to complete projects faster. It is worth the investment if you intend doing a lot of sewing. Take some time to read your sewing machine manual and become familiar with the functions before you begin.

Presser feet

The presser foot holds the fabric firmly against the needle plate while the stitch is formed. It is important to use the correct presser foot for the stitch you are using and to test your tension on a scrap of fabric before you begin. Here are a few presser feet that you will find useful.

• General-purpose foot (A) – for general sewing, utility and embroidery stitches on ordinary fabrics.
• Zipper foot (B) – a narrower foot for sewing in zips and piping. The needle can be adjusted to sew on either side.

• Clear view foot (C) – essential for accurate work as it allows you to see where you are stitching. It can be made from clear fabric or cut away. This foot is ideal for working on bulky fabrics and for machine appliqué.

Machine needles

Use an appropriate machine needle for your work and change it frequently – immediately if damaged or bent. It is handy to keep a selection of the most popular needle sizes.

• Size 70 (9) – for silks and fine cottons (A).
• Size 100 (16) – for leather (B).
• Size 90 (14) – for denims, canvas and heavyweight linens (C).

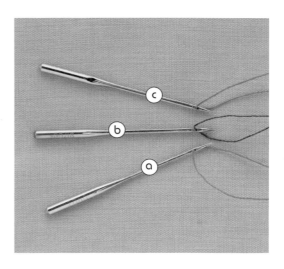

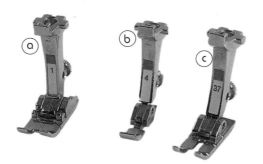

Preparing for machine sewing

Before you begin to stitch, prepare your material. Pinning and tacking (basting) are useful ways of ensuring your fabric is lined up and stays in the correct place when machine sewing.

• Tacking (basting) – tacking fabrics together will ensure that they stay in place as you sew them. Using a thin thread, sew the fabrics together by hand with large running stitches. When you reach the end of the fabric, do not secure the thread with a knot but leave a long tail. When it is time to remove tacking, use an unpicker tool or a pin to pull out the stitches.

• Pinning – you can use pins to sew two fabrics together by machine without tacking (basting). Place the fabrics together, edge to edge. Insert the pins at right angles to the edges of the fabrics, leaving a small gap between the pins. Stitch slowly over the pins – the needle will slip over each pin without bending them. Remove the pins when stitching is complete.

Machine stitches

The type of machine you have will determine the range of stitches available to you. Listed here are the main stitches that you will need to use on your sewing machine to complete the projects in this book.

• Straight stitch – this stitch is the most widely used to join two pieces of fabric together. It can be used for sewing seams and topstitching. For ordinary fabric, set your stitch length to 3mm (⅛in) for tidy, even stitches. For fine fabrics use a shorter stitch length, and increase the stitch length for heavier fabrics.

• Zigzag – this is a versatile stitch, used to neaten seams and edges, as a decorative edge and to hold appliqué motifs in place. To neaten seams, it is best to set your zigzag stitch to 2mm (³⁄₃₂in) in width and length. When using for appliqué, set your zigzag to 2mm (³⁄₃₂in) and between 0.5 and 1mm (³⁄₃₂–¹⁄₁₆in) in length.

• Topstitching – this is a short straight stitch normally sewn about 3mm (⅛in) from the edge of a seam to keep it flat and neat. It can be both decorative and functional, while holding the seam firmly in place. Place the presser foot onto the edge of the seam and use this as a guide to keep the stitching line straight.

Sewing a seam by machine

One of the most basic tasks in any sewing project is sewing a seam. The following techniques use a 1.3cm (½in) seam allowance, which can be adjusted for each project as necessary.

Tack (baste) or pin the seam across the seam line, with the right sides of your fabric together. Place your fabric under the presser foot so that the edge of the seam is next to the 1.3cm (½in) line on the needle plate and the fabric is 6mm (¼in) behind the needle. Use the hand wheel to take the needle down into the fabric, and then begin to sew. Sew at a comfortable speed, guiding the fabric along the 1.3cm (½in) line on the needle plate.

Finished seams can be neatened to prevent them from fraying and weakening. A small, narrow machine zigzag along the raw edges is one of the fastest – try different stitch lengths and widths to find which suits the fabric best. Trim the seam to 6mm (¼in) and zigzag both edges together.

Turning corners

This is a basic skill that is essential when sewing more than one side of a project. Stitch down the first length, leaving a 1.3cm (½in) seam allowance. Slow down as you approach the corner and use the hand wheel to complete the last few stitches. Stop 1.3cm (½in) from the edge, with the needle in the fabric. Lift the presser foot and turn the fabric around so the next seam is lined up with the guideline on the needle plate. Lower the presser foot and continue to sew.

Appliqué

Appliqué is the name for the technique of attaching fabric shapes to other fabrics and the easiest way to do this is with a product called fusible web. This has various trade names, including Bondaweb, WonderWeb, Wonder Under and Vliesofix. It comes in a roll or in pre-cut pieces and looks like paper. One side can be drawn on (so you can trace the shape you want) and the other has a thin membrane of glue that melts when heated by an iron, so allowing two fabrics to be glued together. Designs traced onto fusible web will come out in reverse, so if you don't want this then you will need to flip the tracing first. Be careful to iron only the paper side, otherwise the glue will stick to your iron. If this happens, use an iron cleaner to remove it.

Using fusible web – method 1

1. Use a hot iron to fuse the fusible web on to the back of the fabric you wish to appliqué. Pin the template to the front of the backed fabric and cut out the shape. Straight scissors can be used.

2. Carefully peel the backing paper away, position the motif on the base fabric and press with a hot iron for several seconds to fuse it in position.

Using fusible web – method 2

1. Trace the shape you want on to the paper side of the fusible web. Cut out roughly around this shape and then iron it on to the back of the fabric you wish to appliqué.

2. Carefully cut out the shape and peel off the paper backing. Place the shape on to the base fabric and use a medium to hot iron for several seconds to fuse it in position.

Hand appliqué

For thin fabrics using fusible web will be sufficient to hold the stitches in place. However, when using cotton fabrics for appliqué, extra stitching will be required in addition to the fusible web. Decorative stitches such as running stitch, catch stitch and blanket stitch are all perfect for the job.

Here the butterfly motif is secured with blanket stitch and other simple embroidery stitches have been used for additional decoration.

Machine appliqué

Using a machine straight stitch or a close-set zigzag stitch or satin stitch to apply a fabric motif is an alternative to hand stitching. This will give a secure and durable finish that is ideal for items that will be washed frequently.

Stitching curves

When working on curved motifs, stop on the outside edge, needle down, foot up, and then turn the fabric. To ensure a neat result, it is better to stop and start several times than try to get around the corner in one attempt.

Here the fabric motif is secured by carefully stitching around its outside edge with a machine zigzag stitch set at 2mm (³⁄₃₂in) width and 0.5mm–1mm (¹⁄₆₄–¹⁄₃₂in) length.

The heart appliqué is held in place with machine straight stitch. The less than perfect stitching adds to the charm.

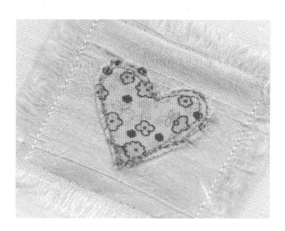

papercraft techniques

Many of the party projects that feature in this book use basic paper-sculpting techniques. To get the best results you need to use the recommended paper weight, measure precisely before you begin, and cut or score carefully.

Making a card blank

Greetings card blanks can be bought ready-made but it's so easy to make your own, which will also give you a much wider choice of card colour, weight and texture. Choose your card colour and a weight heavy enough so the card will stand upright.

1. Decide on the size of your finished card and cut a piece of card this height and twice the width. Make two pencil marks halfway along the width, at the top and bottom, where you want the card to fold. Score a line between these marks using an empty ballpoint pen or a scoring tool.

2. Use both hands to neatly fold the card along the score line, using a bone folder or the back of a metal spoon to create a firm crease.

Tearing paper

Hand-torn paper strips are a good way to decorate a card blank: tear towards you and the white core of the paper makes an attractive edge; tear away from you and no white edge is seen.

Scoring paper

A simple way to add dimension and modelling to a flat piece of paper is to score it. Scoring simply means cutting halfway through the paper before you fold it, enabling paper to be folded precisely and cleanly. This gives the form sharply defined shadows when light falls upon it and makes it three-dimensional. The paper will bend away from the scored line, so scoring can be carried out on either side of the paper.

1. Place your paper on a flat surface, with the correct side for scoring facing up. Draw a faint pencil guideline, then place a metal safety ruler against the line. Draw the back of the wrong side of a craft-knife blade along the score line, pressing just hard enough to break the surface of the paper but not to cut right through it. Be sure to keep your fingers away from the craft-knife blade.

2. Take the paper in both hands and squeeze very gently along the score line, widening the split. Once you have opened the scored line to the end, fold along the score and crease firmly.

3. To score a curved shape, lightly draw a score line down the centre of the paper, following the curve of the shape. Once the paper is scored, squeeze gently along the line to shape the paper and make it three-dimensional.

Curling paper

Paper may be curled in several ways, tightly or loosely, depending on its weight and the size of the piece. Paper, like fabric, has a definite grain, and it is much easier to curl it with the grain. Take a sample of the paper and tear it in half. If it leaves a ragged edge and is difficult to control, you are tearing against the grain. If it tears easily, with a smooth line, you are tearing with the grain.

Curling light/medium-weight strips

To tightly curl narrow strips of lightweight to medium-weight paper and lightweight card, hold firmly in one hand and pull the paper over the closed blades of a pair of scissors. Don't pull thin paper too hard or it will tear.

Curling heavier paper and card

Find the grain of the paper first and then roll it tightly, with the grain, around a pencil. Hold in place for a few seconds to keep the shape.

Rolling paper

To give paper a gently rolled effect, hold it firmly in one hand and pull along the length between finger and thumb several times. It can then be curved into whatever shape you need, and will fold into gentle waves with ease.

Making cones

Curving and overlapping the sides of a flat shape will raise its surface and make it 3D. Circles that are treated in this way become cones.

1. Draw a circle to the required size on paper and cut it out. Snip a straight line from the edge to the centre of the circle.

2. Gently curl the paper by pulling it between finger and thumb so that the surface rises slightly.

3. Curve the edges of the circle around on top of each other until the cone is the desired height. Draw a line where the edges overlap. Spread glue on the edges and press together, overlapping where marked.

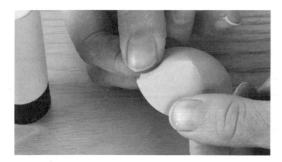

Making concertina pleats

This decorative effect works best with lightweight and medium-weight paper and lightweight card – anything heavier gets unsightly creases when it is pleated.

1. Mark the width of the pleats along the top and bottom edge of both sides of the paper. Remember to alternate the spacing of the lines on the front and back to achieve a concertina effect when the paper is folded.

2. Lay the paper out flat. Place your ruler vertically, joining up each corresponding pair of marks, and score between them. Turn the paper over and repeat on the other side.

3. Carefully pleat the paper, pinching along the scored lines to open them before each fold is made.

Making tabbed walls

Using tabbed walls is the easiest way to make a shape three-dimensional, such as the Cupcake Boxes. A paper or card strip is snipped into tabs and scored along one or both sides. These can then be manipulated to follow curves, circles and other shapes. Tabs can then be glued to the shape to create a side, or glued to join two shapes if tabbed on both sides.

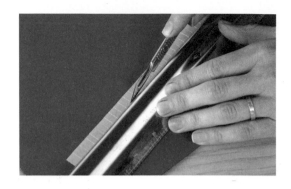

1. Cut the strip to the width and length required. Draw a 1–1.5cm (³/₈–⁵/₈in) deep border along one or both sides. Snip carefully along the wall as far as the border, approximately every 1.5cm (⁵/₈in).

2. Place the wall right side up on a cutting mat. Score along the border with the wrong side of a craft knife blade. Fold under the tabs.

3. To attach the wall to a curved shape, curl it between finger and thumb to make it pliable. Spread glue on the tabs and curve the wall around your shape, matching the wall to the profile of the shape as precisely as possible. Press down the tabs, trim the wall to size and finally, glue and overlap the ends.

Making a lidded box

This baker's style cake box is perfect for presenting a single cupcake, or make it larger to hold several. See Templates for diagrams for making the two sizes of box. They are quick and easy to make, and strong yet lightweight.

1. Cut the box from lightweight card. Place the card on a cutting mat and carefully score the fold lines where marked. Fold up the sides where marked and fold the tabs inwards. Crease all the fold lines firmly so that the sides stand upright.

2. Spread a thin layer of PVA (white) glue on to the tabs or attach strips of double-sided tape. Position the tabs against the box sides, making sure that the edges match exactly. Press the tabs to secure.

Stitching paper

You can use machine stitching to hold paper together but at the same time create a really interesting visual effect as on the Handbag Gift Bag. Stitching on paper is simple to do and in fact is easier than sewing fabric because there are no frayed edges to deal with.

1. You can't pin two pieces of paper together without marking them, but they will slide around and move if they are not held together in some way. The solution is to use small pieces of masking tape to keep the paper in place while you sew, which can then be gently peeled off afterwards.

2. Use a long straight stitch and a fairly thick needle – one that is designed for use on denim or leather is ideal. Sew carefully and slowly, and

when you reach a corner, stop the machine, lift the presser foot and turn the paper before continuing to sew. If you try to turn it while stitching, the paper may tear.

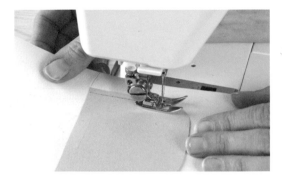

3. To finish off a row of stitching, lift the presser foot, remove the paper and cut the threads, leaving long ends. Turn the paper face down and pull the top thread through to the back with a pin. Tie the ends of the thread tightly and trim.

sugarcraft techniques

This section will be very useful for those new to sugarcraft. It includes some basic cake and cookie recipes, and has everything you need to know about colouring and modelling with sugarpaste to create, sweet, stunning centrepieces for any party table. Whether you are planning on making the Cocktail Cookies for an elegant drinks party, the Swirl Cupcakes for a wedding reception, or the Hedgehog Cake for a child's birthday party, there are a few basics – equipment and recipes – that you can't do without.

Baking essentials

Large electric mixer – For making cakes, buttercream and royal icing.

Kitchen scales – For weighing out ingredients.
Measuring spoons – For small quantities.

Mixing bowls – For mixing ingredients.
Spatulas – For mixing and gently folding together cake mixes.

Cake tins – For baking cakes.

Bun tray/ muffin tray – For baking cupcakes.

Baking trays – For baking cookies.

Wire racks – For cooling cakes.

Baking cookies

Cookies are great fun to make for just about any occasion. You can cut out any shapes from the cookie dough and decorate them however you like. This dough can be made up to two weeks ahead or stored in the freezer until ready to use.

you will need (makes 10–15 large or 25–30 medium cookies) ...

- 250g (9oz) unsalted butter
- 250g (9oz) caster (superfine) sugar
- 1–2 medium eggs
- 1 teaspoon vanilla extract
- 500g (1lb 2oz) plain (all-purpose) flour

For different flavour variations it is easy to modify the basic cookie recipe.

For chocolate cookies substitute 50g (1¾oz) flour with cocoa powder (unsweetened cocoa).

For citrus cookies add the finely grated zest of one lemon or orange.

For almond cookies replace the vanilla extract with 1 teaspoon almond extract.

1. Beat the butter and sugar together until creamy and quite fluffy. Add the eggs and vanilla extract and mix until they are well combined.

2. Sift the flour, add to the bowl and mix until all the ingredients just come together. You may need to do this in two stages – do not over-mix.

3. Tip the dough into a container lined with clingfilm (plastic wrap) and press down firmly. Cover with clingfilm and refrigerate for at least 30 minutes.

4. On a work surface lightly dusted with flour, roll out the cookie dough to about 4mm (⅛in) thick. Sprinkle a little extra flour on top of the dough as you roll to prevent it from sticking to the rolling pin.

5. Cut out your shapes using your cutters. Place on baking trays lined with greaseproof (wax) paper and return to the fridge to rest for at least 30 minutes.

6. Bake the cookies in a preheated oven at 180°C/350°F/Gas Mark 4 for about 10 minutes, depending on their size, or until they are golden brown. Leave them to cool completely before storing them in an airtight container until you are ready to decorate them.

Baking classic chocolate cake

This recipe for the Streamers Cake is really quick and easy to make and has a lovely light texture. Although the method is the same for both the 13cm (5in) and 20cm (8in) round cakes, the quantities for the ingredients will obviously differ.

you will need (for the 13cm/5in round cake) ...

- 170g (6oz) plain (all purpose) flour
- 30g (1oz) cocoa powder (unsweetened cocoa)
- 1 1/2 teaspoons baking powder
- 150g (5½oz) unsalted butter
- 130g (4½oz) caster (superfine) sugar
- 2½ large eggs
- 100ml (3½fl oz) full-fat (whole) milk

you will need (for the 20cm/8in round cake) ...

- 365g (12½oz) plain (all purpose) flour
- 65g (2¼oz) cocoa powder (unsweetened cocoa)
- 3¼ teaspoons baking powder
- 325g (11½oz) unsalted butter
- 285g (10oz) caster (superfine) sugar
- 5 large eggs
- 220ml (8fl oz) full-fat (whole) milk

1. Preheat your oven to 160°C/325°F/Gas Mark 3, and grease and line your tins.

2. Sift the flour, cocoa powder and baking powder together.

3. Beat the butter and sugar together until light and fluffy. Crack your eggs into a separate bowl. Add the eggs to the mixture gradually, beating well between each addition.

4. Add half the dry ingredients and mix until just combined before adding half the milk. Repeat with the remaining ingredients. Mix until the mixture starts to come together; finish mixing with a spatula and spoon into your prepared tins.

5. Bake in the oven until a skewer inserted into the centre of your cakes comes out clean. Check smaller cakes after 20 minutes and larger cakes after 40 minutes.

6. Leave to cool, then wrap the cakes well in clingfilm and refrigerate until ready to use.

The ingredients for the 13cm (5in) round cake can be used to make 10–12 cupcakes. Place your cupcake cases in a bun tray (muffin pan) and fill them half to two-thirds only.

Baking moist chocolate cake

The recipe for the Hedgehog Cake differs slightly from the Streamers Cake and produces a rich, moist, yet firm, chocolate cake. The secret to success is to use good-quality chocolate with a reasonably high cocoa solids content; luxury plain Belgian chocolate with a cocoa solid content of around 50% works well. The ingredients given are for a 25.5 x 20cm (10 x 8in) rectangular chocolate cake.

you will need ...

- 500g (1lb 2oz) plain (semisweet) chocolate, chopped
- 350g (12oz) unsalted butter
- 225g (8oz) caster (superfine) sugar
- 12 large eggs
- 75g (3oz) icing (confectioners') sugar
- 350g (12oz) self-raising flour

1. Preheat your oven to 180°C/350°F/Gas Mark 4, and grease and line your tin.

2. Melt the chocolate in a heatproof bowl over a pan of simmering water or in a microwave. Cream the butter and sugar in a large mixing bowl until light, fluffy and pale.

3. Separate the eggs. Gradually add the egg yolks, then the melted chocolate. In a separate bowl, whisk the egg whites to soft peaks. Gradually whisk the icing sugar into the egg whites.

4. Sift the flour into another bowl and, using a large metal spoon, gently fold the flour alternately with the egg whites into the chocolate mixture.

5. Transfer the mixture into the lined tin and bake for approx. 1½–1¾ hours. When the cake is baked it will be well risen, firm to the touch and a skewer inserted into the centre will come out clean.

6. Leave the cake to cool completely in the tin; then, leaving the lining paper on top, wrap the cake in foil or place in an airtight container for at least 12 hours before cutting, to allow the cake to settle.

Buttercream

Buttercream can be stored in an airtight container until required. Use it to sandwich cakes together or to coat them before covering with sugarpaste.

you will need (to make one quantity) ...

- 110g (3¾oz) unsalted butter
- 350g (12oz) icing (confectioners') sugar

1. Place the butter in a bowl and beat until the mixture is light and fluffy.

2. Sift in the icing sugar and continue to beat until the mixture changes colour and is a firm, spreadable consistency.

Tempering chocolate

Chocolate contains cocoa butter crystals and tempering is a process of heating chocolate so that these crystals are uniform. Correctly tempered chocolate will produce an end result that is smooth-tasting, crisp, even-coloured and shiny, while incorrectly tempered chocolate produces a dull or streaky end result often referred to as a 'bloom', which while not inedible, does look unsightly and will taste grainy. Incorrectly tempered chocolate will not set very well, will 'bend' rather than 'snap', and will not release easily from moulds, so before placing chocolate into a mould ensure it is correctly tempered.

How to temper chocolate

The simplest method is to purchase chocolate couverture callets or buttons, which have already been through one of the processes of tempering. With extreme care, these can be melted in a small plastic bowl in the microwave in short 10 second bursts on full power (850w), mixing thoroughly between each interval.

For chocolate buttercream, first add 2 tablespoons of cocoa powder (unsweetened cocoa) to 1–2 tablespoons of milk, then add just enough of this mixture to the buttercream to maintain its firm spreadable consistency.

Sugarpaste and modelling paste

Sugarpaste is available in many different colours. However, to get exact shades, you can use colouring paste to colour white sugarpaste. Place a little paste colour onto the end of a cocktail stick (toothpick) or a larger amount onto the end of a palette knife. Add to the paste and knead in thoroughly, adding more until you have the correct result. Be careful with pale colours, as only a little colour is needed.

Modelling paste is basically a stiffer version of sugarpaste that enables you to mould larger, less delicate shapes. It isn't as strong and won't dry out as quickly. You can buy ready-made modelling paste, but it is really simple and cheaper to make your own using CMC. This is a powder that is kneaded into the sugarpaste; use about 1 teaspoon per 300g (10½oz) icing.

Covering a round cake

To achieve a neat appearance for your finished cake it pays to take a little time to achieve a perfectly smooth finish.

1. To level off the cake place a cake board into the base of the tin in which the cake was baked so that when the cake is placed on top the outer edge of the cake is level with the tin and the dome will protrude above. Take a long sharp knife and cut the dome from the cake, keeping the knife against the tin. This will ensure the cake is completely level.

2. Cut the sponge into layers if you wish to add a filling. Using a small palette knife, spread a small amount of buttercream onto the cake board and stick down the bottom layer. Fill your cake layer(s) with buttercream and jam if you are using.

3. Cover the sides and top of the layered cake with a thin, even layer of buttercream. Refrigerate for at least an hour before covering with sugarpaste.

4. Knead the sugarpaste until it is soft. Roll it out with a large non-stick rolling pin on a large non-stick board, set over a non-stick mat. Use spacers to give you the correct depth – about 5mm (¾in). Try to keep the shape round so that it will fit over your cake easily

6. When the icing is on, use a smoother in a circular motion to go over the top of the cake. For the side of the cake, go around in forward circular movements, almost cutting the excess paste at the base. Trim the excess with a small, sharp knife and smooth once more.

5. Pick the sugarpaste up on your rolling pin and lay it over your cake. Quickly but carefully use your hands to smooth it around and down the side of the cake. Pull the sugarpaste away from the side of the cake as you go until you reach the base. Try to push out any air bubbles that may occur.

Icing cake boards

Covering the base cake board with sugarpaste makes a huge difference to the finished cake. By carefully choosing the right colour for the icing, the board can be incorporated into the design of the cake itself.

Moisten the board with some water. Roll out the sugarpaste to 4mm (a generous ⅛in). Pick the icing up on the rolling pin and lay it over the cake board. Place the board either on a turntable or bring it towards the edge of the work surface so that the icing is hanging down over it. Use your smoother in a downwards motion to cut a smooth edge around the board. Cut away any excess. Finish by smoothing the top using circular movements to achieve a flat and perfectly smooth surface for your cake to sit on. Leave to dry overnight.

Assembling tiered cakes

Stacking cakes on top of one another is not a difficult process, but it needs to be done in the right way so that you can rest assured that the cake is structurally sound. For a round cake a minimum of three hollow plastic dowels are required. These are very sturdy and easily cut to the correct height.

1. Mark the cake where the dowels should go. These need to be positioned well inside the diameter of the cake to be stacked on top. Push a dowel into the cake where it has been marked. Using an edible pen, mark the dowel where it meets the top of the cake.

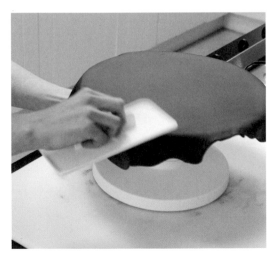

2. Remove the dowel and cut it at the mark with a serrated knife. Cut the other dowels to the same height and insert them all into the cake.

4. Stick your base cake onto the centre of your iced cake board with some stiff royal icing. Allow the icing to set for a few minutes before stacking on the next tier.

3. Place a cake board on top of the dowels and check that they are equal in height by using a spirit level.

templates

The following templates have been reduced in size. They will all need to be enlarged on a photocopier by 200%.

Using templates

Many of the projects in this book have templates for you to trace or photocopy and transfer to fabric or paper, and these are presented on the pages that follow. For the paper sculpted projects please refer to the key on this page for advice on scoring and cutting, and follow the coloured guidelines when using the templates as explained below.

1. A green solid score line indicates that the scoring is to be done on the front of the paper. Transfer the outline of the template and the solid lines to the paper and cut out the shape Score along the solid lines.

2. A blue broken score line indicates that the scoring is to be done on the back of the paper. Turn the shape over, then transfer the broken lines to the paper and score them in the same way.

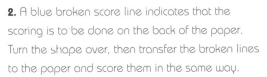

3. When you have completed the scoring, press along the edges on the front and back to crease the paper and make it three-dimensional.

Pink Tiara

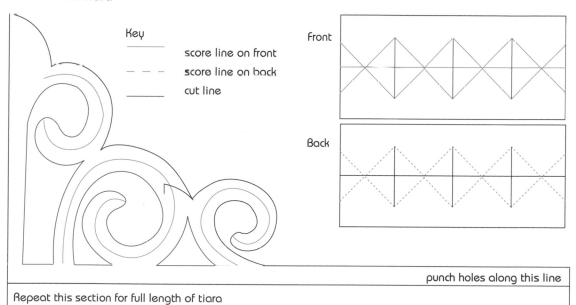

Key

——————— score line on front

- - - - - - - score line on back

——————— cut line

Front

Back

punch holes along this line

Repeat this section for full length of tiara

base

Cocktail Glasses

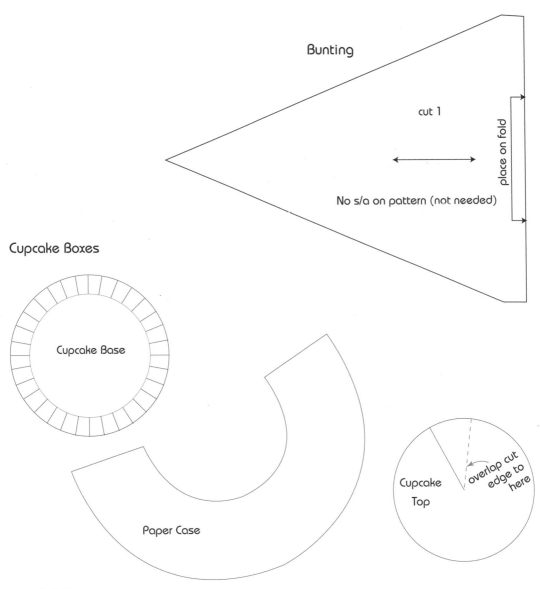

Bunting

cut 1

place on fold

No s/a on pattern (not needed)

Cupcake Boxes

Cupcake Base

Paper Case

Cupcake
Top

overlap cut
edge to
here

Hedgehog Cake

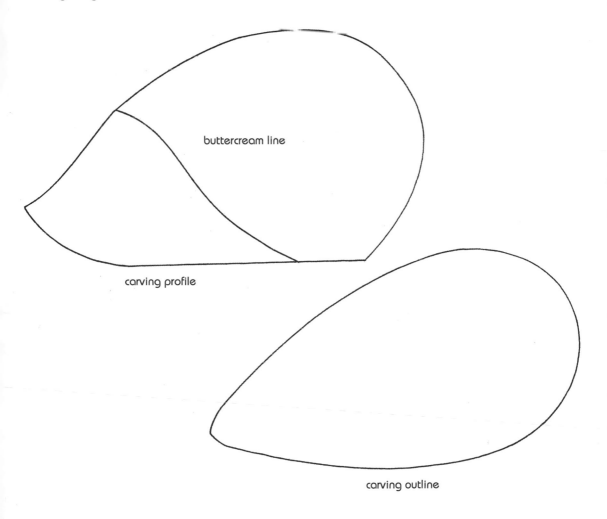

buttercream line

carving profile

carving outline

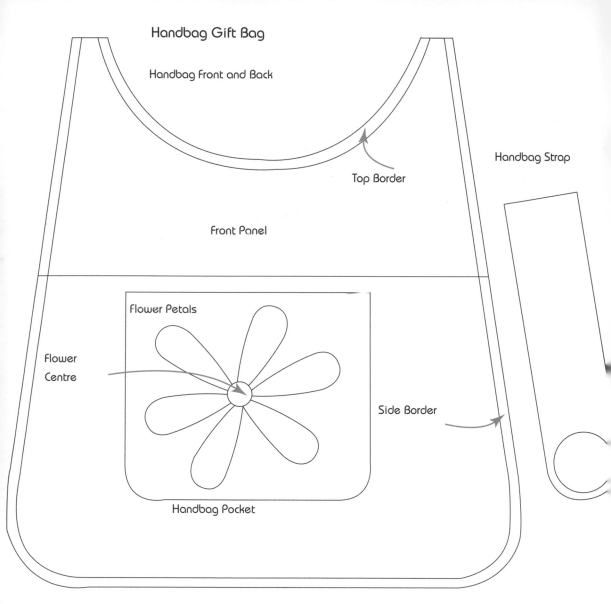

Handbag Gift Bag

Handbag Front and Back

Handbag Strap

Top Border

Front Panel

Flower Petals

Flower Centre

Side Border

Handbag Pocket

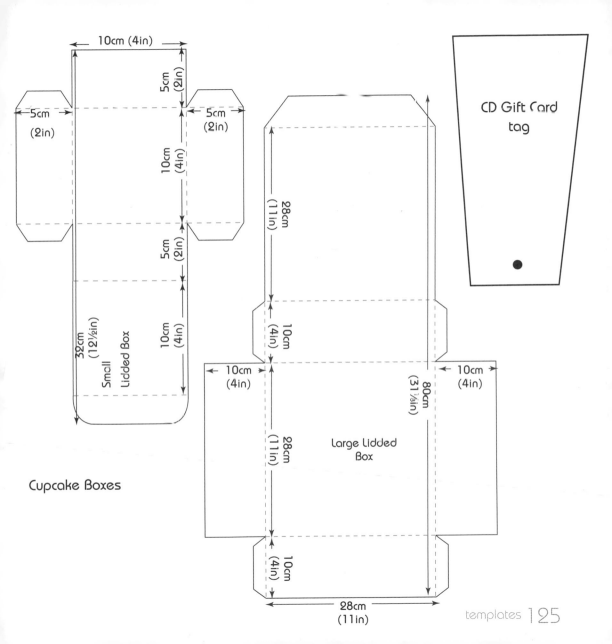

10cm (4in)

5cm (2in)

5cm (2in)

5cm (2in)

10cm (4in)

5cm (2in)

32cm (12½in)   Small Lidded Box

10cm (4in)

Cupcake Boxes

28cm (11in)

10cm (4in)

10cm (4in)

10cm (4in)

80cm (31⅛in)

28cm (11in)

Large Lidded Box

10cm (4in)

28cm (11in)

CD Gift Card tag

designer credits

The publishers would like to thank the following designers who have allowed the reproduction of their designs in this book.

Paper Lanterns
Marion Elliot

Cupcake Napkin
Alice Butcher & Ginny Farquhar

Elegant Garlands
Marion Elliot

3D Paper Letters
Marion Elliot

Cocktail Glasses
Dorothy Wood

Pink Tiara
Marion Elliot

Celebration Bunting
Alice Butcher & Ginny Farquhar

Cocktail Cookies
Lindy Smith

Swirl Cupcakes
Lindy Smith

Streamers Cake
Zoe Clark

Present Cookies
Lindy Smith

Smiley Lollipops
Tracey Mann

Hedgehog Cake
Lindy Smith

Animal Cupcakes
Lindy Smith

Balloons Pop-Up Card
Joanne Sanderson

Beaded Gift Bags
Dorothy Wood

Handbag Gift Bag
Marion Elliot

Mirrored Gift Boxes
Ellen Kharade

Gift Token Card
Marion Elliot

Beaded Star Cards
Dorothy Wood

Cupcake Boxes
Marion Elliot

index

A DAVID & CHARLES BOOK

© F&W Media International, Ltd 2012

David & Charles is an imprint of
F&W Media International, Ltd
Brunel House, Forde Close, Newton Abbot, TQ12 4PU, UK

F&W Media International, Ltd is a
subsidiary of F+W Media, Inc
10151 Carver Road, Cincinnati OH45242, USA

First published in the UK and US in 2012
Digital edition published in 2012

Layout of digital editions may vary depending
on reader hardware and display settings.

The authors and publisher have made every effort
to ensure that all the instructions in the book are
accurate and safe, and therefore cannot accept
liability for any resulting injury, damage or loss
to persons or property, however it may arise.

Names of manufacturers and product ranges are
provided for the information of readers, with no
intention to infringe copyright or trademarks.

A catalogue record for this book is
available from the British Library.

ISBN-13: 978-1-4463-0230-9 hardback
ISBN-10: 1-4463-0230-X hardback

ISBN-13: 978-1-4463-5643-2 e-pub
ISBN-10: 1-4463-5643-4 e-pub

ISBN-13: 978-1-4463-5642-5 PDF
ISBN-10: 1-4463-5642-6 PDF

Hardback edition printed in China by RR Donnelley for:
F&W Media International, Ltd
Brunel House, Forde Close, Newton Abbot, TQ12 4PU, UK

10 9 8 7 6 5 4 3 2 1

Desk Editor: Jeni Hennah
Assistant Editor: Grace Harvey
Project Editor: Cheryl Brown
Design Manager: Sarah Clark
Photographers: Sian Irvine, Karl Adamson,
Simon Whitmore, Kim Sayer
Senior Production Controller: Kelly Smith

F+W Media publishes high quality books
on a wide range of subjects.
For more great book ideas visit: **www.rucraft.co.uk**

loved this book?

Why not visit our website to tell us what you think?

www.lovethisbook.co.uk

Make Me I'm Yours... Sewing

Various

ISBN-13: 978-0-7153-3772-1

Discover the pleasure of sewing with this stylish collection of 20 gorgeous, simple-to-make projects. Choose from a selection of chic designs, including bags, gifts and cushions.

Make Me I'm Yours... Just for Fun

Various

ISBN-13: 978-1-4463-0069-5

Be inspired to get crafty with this diverse collection of 20 fabulous projects. Create unique gifts and accessories, from jewellery and bags to socks, photo frames and various fun items for yourself and your home!

Make Me I'm Yours... Christmas

Various

ISBN-13: 978-0-7153-3896-4

Celebrate Christmas in style by creating unique and special items for yourself, friends and family. Fill your home with gorgeous handmade decorations, gifts, cards and edible treats for the festive period.

Make Me I'm Yours... Cushions

Various

ISBN-13: 978 1-4463 0145-6

A selection of over 15 soft and cosy projects, including pillows, scented sachets, pincushions and other adorable items. Personalize your designs with funky embellishments and decorative stitches to match your home and furniture.